Dolphins! A Kid Amazing Pictures and Fun Facts About Dolphins

By John Yost

Copyright © 2018

All rights reserved

Please respect my copyright of this book. You may use this eBook for your personal enjoyment. Just like a printed book, I encourage you share it with family and friends. But please don't change or modify this book in any way.

Your personal license to enjoy this book doesn't extend to reselling or redistributing this book in whole or part for any other commercial purpose. In all other respects you are invited to enjoy and share this book with family, friends and other loved ones.

Please spread the word and support John by encouraging others to purchase and enjoy this book and others in his Nature Books for Children series.

Table of Contents

INTRODUCTION 4

ANATOMY 8

SENSES 12

FEEDING AND HUNTING 14

BEHAVIOR 16

CAREERS WITH DOLPHINS 19

DIFFERENT KINDS OF DOLPHINS 22

AMAZON RIVER DOLPHINS 22

BOTTLENOSE DOLPHINS 26

ORCAS 28

A NOTE FROM JOHN 30

Introduction

Dolphins are amazing animals. They swim like fish, but they are not fish. They are mammals—marine mammals to be exact.

All mammals are warm-blooded, have a backbone, and give birth to live babies. Marine mammals live in the ocean.

Dolphins live in oceans all over the world, but you find them only near the surface of the water. Dolphins breathe above the water like you do when you go swimming.

A dolphin has lungs and breathes through a hole on top of its head. This would be like you having your nose on top of your head!

Dolphins breathe air above the water and can stay underwater for only 15 minutes before they have to come up for air.

Dolphins live all over the world. You can find them in each of the five oceans: Pacific, Atlantic, Indian, Antarctic, and Arctic. Some dolphins can even be found in rivers.

There are about 30 kinds of dolphins. The largest is the orca, also known as the killer whale. Yes, killer whales are actually dolphins!

The killer whale is the biggest dolphin in the world.

Dolphins are closely related to whales. Many sea creatures more than 9 feet long are called "whales" even if they are not really whales.

Real whales are called "baleen whales," because they have no teeth. They filter their food through baleen, which are kind of like the bristles on a broom.

Whales have two blowholes. Dolphins have only one blowhole and dolphins have teeth, which makes them different from whales.

Dolphins are closely related to porpoises too. You can usually tell the difference by looking at their noses. Dolphins have long beaks, and porpoises have round noses.

Dolphins have curved dorsal fins on their backs, and porpoises have dorsal fins shaped like triangles. Dolphins are much larger than porpoises as well.

If you see a marine mammal and you don't know if it's a dolphin or a porpoise, it's probably a dolphin. There are many more dolphins in the oceans compared to porpoises.

Because there are lots of different kinds of dolphins, they come in many sizes. Male dolphins are almost always larger than the females. The males are called *bulls* and the females are called *cows*. A baby dolphin is called a *calf*.

Anatomy

Dolphins are usually between eight feet and 20 feet long. The smallest dolphin is Maui's dolphin, it is only four feet long and weighs about 90 pounds. The killer whale is the largest dolphin and can be over 25 feet long. Killer whales weigh more than 20,000 pounds!

Dolphins have to stay warm in the cold ocean water. They have a big, thick layer of fat called *blubber*. The fatty blubber insulates the dolphin and keeps it warm. Blubber is also used instead of food when the dolphin can't find anything to eat. Dolphins that live in the coldest waters have the thickest blubber.

If you look at the pictures in this book carefully, you might notice that dolphins are darker on their backs and lighter on their bellies. This is called *countershading* and it is a type of camouflage. From above the dolphin is harder to see because it blends in with the dark ocean floor. From underneath dolphins are hard to see because they blend in with the light shining into the water.

Dolphins are darker on the top and lighter on the bottom. This "countershading" makes them harder to see.

Usually dolphins are gray, but they come in other colors too. Orcas are black and white. Some dolphins are brown, blue, and some are even bright pink!

To breathe, dolphins swim to the surface of the water. They blow out the old air and breathe in new air, all in less than a second. Muscles shut the blowhole quickly before the dolphin goes back under the water, otherwise the dolphin would drown.

Dolphins have between 80 and 100 teeth. They don't use their teeth for chewing though. Their teeth are round and shaped like cones. They catch prey with their teeth and swallow it whole.

Dolphins have teeth, but they don't use them for chewing.

Dolphins are powerful swimmers. Their tails push them through the water and their front flippers are used for steering. The two sides of a dolphin's tail are called *flukes*. The flukes move up and down and push the dolphin forward at top speeds of up to 30 mph. The dorsal fin on the dolphin's back keeps the dolphin straight so it doesn't spin in circles as it swims.

Dolphins are powerful swimmers and can leap high out of the water.

Some dolphin mothers carry their babies inside them for 9 months, just like human mothers. Other kinds of dolphins carry their babies for almost one and a half years!

Dolphins, like all mammals, take care of their young. A mother dolphin feeds milk to her calf for two years. Usually a cow has only one calf, but sometimes she will have twins. Dolphin babies come out tail first. When the calf is born, the mother lifts her baby above water so the calf can breathe. Calves normally stay with their mothers for 5 years.

Senses

Dolphins see very well. Even dolphins that live in muddy river water have good eyesight. Dolphins are color-blind, but they see both above and below the water. Dolphins see well at night because their eyes collect a lot of light.

Dolphins have tiny ears but their hearing is amazing! Dolphins can hear ten times better than we can. Dolphins also hear high pitched sounds that people can't hear at all.

Every dolphin makes a unique sound like a whistle. Dolphins use these sounds to find each other.

Dolphins have an extra sense called *echolocation*. Echolocation is a kind of sonar. Dolphins send out high frequency sounds at 1,000 clicks per second. These sounds bounce off of things in the water and back to the dolphin. The "echo" the dolphins get back tells them the size, shape, and distance of things around them. Dolphins are not the only animals that use echolocation, bats use it too.

Each dolphin has its own voice and dolphins can tell each other apart by their voices. This helps dolphins find their family and members of their group.

Dolphins are sensitive to *touch*. The blowhole, eyes, snout, and lower jaw are very sensitive.

Dolphins are sensitive to touch, especially around their heads.

Dolphins *taste* the same things we do: salt, bitter, sweet, and sour. But their sense of taste isn't as good as ours. Dolphins suck water into their mouths to taste it. The taste of the water lets dolphins know what is around them. It might tell them predators or prey are nearby. The taste of the water also tells them when another dolphin is ready to mate.

Feeding and Hunting

Dolphins are *carnivores*, which means they eat meat. They have round, cone-shaped teeth, which are no good for tearing or chewing, but are great for holding prey in their jaws before swallowing it whole.

Dolphins swallow their food whole.

What dolphins eat depends a lot on where they live, but dolphins eat lots of fish like cod, mackerel, tuna, catfish, and herring. Dolphins also eat crab, lobsters, turtles, squid, and shrimp.

Big dolphins like the orcas, eat larger animals like seals and sea lions. Sometimes killer whales hunt and eat small whales. When they are really hungry, orcas even attack and eat other dolphins.

When hunting fish, dolphins use a method called *herding*. The dolphins surround a school of fish and make the fish swim closer and closer together.

Then the dolphins take turns diving through the thick school of fish, eating the fish as they swim through the school.

Corralling is when dolphins chase a school of fish to shallow water. The fish get trapped between the dolphins and the shore. When the fish try to swim out to deeper water, the dolphins take turns eating the fish.

Sometimes a dolphin hits a fish with its tail to knock the fish out. Then the dolphin grabs the fish while it's still stunned. This is called *whacking*.

Another way dolphins daze their prey is by sending a very loud sound through the water. The loud noise shocks the fish and confuses it. This method is called *stunning* and it makes the fish easy for the dolphin to catch.

Foraging is a fascinating way some bottlenose dolphins find food. They pick up a sponge and use it to scrape the ocean floor looking for food. The sponge protects the dolphin's beak. Very few animals are smart enough to use tools, and using the sponge as a scraper proves dolphins are very smart.

Behavior

Dolphins are social creatures. They swim in groups and communicate with each other. The groups are called *pods*. Each pod usually has between 15 and 20 dolphins.

Dolphins live together to help them survive. They hunt, eat, keep each other safe, and play together. Dolphins help each other when they are sick. They stay with the sick or injured dolphin, keeping it safe from predators like sharks. They even take the sick dolphin to the water's surface to breathe.

Dolphins live together in groups called "pods."

Sometimes multiple pods come together where there is a lot of food. This group of pods is called a *superpod*. One superpod can have over 1,000 dolphins in it!

To communicate, dolphins use squeaks, clicks, and whistles. They don't make these sounds with their mouths, they make noises with their blowholes.

Believe it or not, dolphins can stay awake for five days straight, but they have to sleep and rest eventually. They also have to come up for air every fifteen minutes, so they fall *half* asleep. They do something called *unihemispheric sleeping,* where only one side of their brain, or *hemisphere,* sleeps at a time. This way their brain can rest, one side at a time. Their bodies rest while they swim slowly.

When they are wide-awake, dolphins are very playful creatures. They splash and make bubbles. They even throw seaweed at each other.

Dolphins are very playful creatures!

Dolphins can jump high out of the water. If they want to go really fast, dolphins jump out of the water over and over. This is called *porpoising*. Sometimes dolphins jump when they are fighting too.

Dolphins can also walk on water. They walk backwards though. They jump out of the water and use their strong tails to "walk" across the top of the water.

Dolphins are caring creatures. They help each other and even help people. Dolphins have lifted drowning people to the surface and saved people from sharks.

Careers With Dolphins

If you love dolphins, there are many jobs that involve working with them.

Dolphin trainers work personally with the animals. They take care of the dolphins, keep them happy, and train them for shows.

Dolphin trainers work with dolphins, take care of them, and teach people about them.

Dolphin trainers need to know a lot about dolphins so they can take good care of them. Trainers also use what they know about dolphins to teach others to respect dolphins. Teaching audiences and answering questions during shows is a big part of their job.

A dolphin trainer might also work with other marine mammals like sea lions, walruses, and whales.

A **zookeeper** is a person who takes care of animals living in a zoo. The part of the zoo with marine animals is called the *aquarium*. Some zookeepers only take care of dolphins and other marine mammals.

A zookeeper working with dolphins feeds, cleans up after, and keeps the dolphins happy.

If you love dolphins, you might enjoy a career that involves working with them.

A **veterinarian**, or *vet* for short, takes care of sick or hurt animals. They are just like your family doctor, except they take care of animals instead of people.

Some vets work only with marine mammals. A marine mammal vet studies the bodies and lives of dolphins and other aquatic mammals. They help sick and injured dolphins, whales, walruses, and other marine mammals.

A **marine biologist** is a scientist who studies animals that live in the ocean or other bodies of water. Being a marine biologist includes a lot of work "in the field," meaning they spend a lot of time in or near water.

Studying dolphins and learning about the way they live helps us protect dolphins.

A marine biologist's day at work includes many things like diving into the ocean, collecting animals, doing experiments, and watching animal behavior. A marine biologist can specialize in studying and learning about dolphins.

Different Kinds of Dolphins

Amazon River Dolphins

The Amazon River in South America is home to the pink dolphin.

What, a pink dolphin?!?

Yes, there are pink dolphins! They live in the Amazon River. The Amazon River dolphin is not the only freshwater dolphin, but it is the largest. It is also known as the "Boto."

The Amazon River has warm water, which could be the reason the Amazon River dolphin has thinner skin than other dolphins. This could also be why it looks pink; you can see its blood vessels through its thin skin.

Female Amazon River dolphins are often larger than the males. Females can be over 8 feet long and weigh over 215 pounds! Males can grow up to 6 and a half feet in length and get as heavy as 200 pounds.

Amazon River dolphins are famous because of their pink skin, but not all of them are pink. They can also be different shades of gray, white, yellow, and brown.

Not all "pink" dolphins are actually pink.

Amazon River dolphins have a hump on their back instead of a dorsal fin. They have a long, thin nose. These dolphins are not fast, but they are very flexible. They can stretch so much that they can turn their heads halfway around!

They have small eyes and can't see much in the muddy water. They use echolocation to find food.

Dolphins are usually the predator and not the prey. But animals like caimans (a kind of alligator), jaguars, and anacondas eat Amazon River dolphins.

The Amazon River dolphin is considered a "vulnerable species." That means there are not many of these dolphins left in the world. Human pollution, boat traffic and people scaring the dolphins away make it hard for the dolphins to survive in the wild.

Bottlenose Dolphins

When you think of dolphins, the bottlenose dolphins are probably the type you think of. They are the most common kind of dolphin.

The bottlenose dolphin is the most well-known dolphin.

You see bottlenose dolphins at Sea World because they are so smart and easy to train. People love dolphins, maybe because of their curved mouths which make them look like they are smiling.

People love dolphins, and dolphins like people too!

The nose of a bottlenose dolphin looks like the neck of a bottle. This is how it got its name. A dolphin's nose is called a *beak*. Bottlenose dolphins have a beak about 3 inches long.

Their whole body is about as long as a car. They are usually 9-12 feet long and weigh about 500 pounds. They are charcoal gray on top and have white bellies.

Bottlenose dolphins like warm water, so they are found in tropical waters. They will travel to find food or warmer water, but otherwise they don't travel much.

Because dolphins are social animals, they always live in groups, called *pods*. Bottlenose dolphins are no different. Sometimes there are only two of them swimming together, but usually there are 10-15 dolphins in a pod.

Bottlenose dolphins "talk" to each other, but not with words. Each dolphin makes its own whistling sound. Dolphins can tell each other apart by the sound of the whistle. Dolphins also communicate by slapping their tails on the water. This lets other dolphins know there is danger around or that there is food close by.

Orcas

Orcas are also known as "killer whales."

Even though it is better known by the name *killer whale*, the orca is a kind of dolphin.

Orcas are found in every ocean. They even live in the extremely cold Antarctic and Arctic Oceans. They are black with white chests and sides and white patches around their eyes. The babies are born with a yellow or orange tint, but this changes to white as the calves get older.

The orca is the largest kind of dolphin. Male orcas are 20 to 26 feet long and can weigh up to 22,000 pounds!

Female orcas are a little smaller than males. They are from 16 to 23 feet long and weigh about 16,500 pounds.

Orcas are the fastest of all marine mammals. They can swim up to 34 miles per hour!

Orcas are *apex predators*. That means they are at the top of the food chain and nothing eats them. Humans are their only threat.

Orcas aren't picky eaters. They eat small animals like tuna, mackerel, shrimp, and turtles. They also eat big animals such as sea lions, walruses, and even whales. Orcas have been known to eat other dolphins as well.

Orcas are very social and travel with their families. Most male orcas never leave their mothers. Each pod, or family, of orcas has its own clicks, whistles, and squeaks they use to communicate.

Orcas are very social and travel hundreds of miles with their families.

Female orcas have babies until they are 40 years old. Most females have about four or five babies in her lifetime. Orcas can live to be 90 years old.

Because there are so few of them, orcas are listed on the endangered list.

A Note From John

Dear Reader,

Thank you very much for reading my book on dolphins. I get great feedback from teachers, parents, and children who have enjoyed my books. I hope you like this book on dolpihns!

If you enjoyed this book, please leave me a 5 Star review on Amazon. Your review really helps me out a lot! :) You can leave your 5 Star review.

This book about dolphins is the fifth in a series of Nature Books for Children. I'm excited to write this series for you and your loved ones.

As a child, I grew up running wild in rural Wisconsin where I discovered mystery after mystery. My summers were spent exploring nature and biking to town so I could look things up at the library.

I would pour over the books in the 599 section (remember the Dewy Decimal System?) searching for answers to the questions I had about the things I'd seen out in the woods, fields, and streams.

My love for animals continued in college where I got a degree in animal science and received my Teaching Certification. For the next eight years, I taught high school science.

During that time, I lived in a tiny log cabin I built myself in the middle of the woods. I had no running water, no electricity and no TV.

Every day I would journal about my life and the animals around my cabin. Much of this series is based on my time there and my love for nature.

Now, I get to pass on a life-time of love, teaching, and learning to children all over the world. I truly hope you are inspired to appreciate this beautiful world we live in.

Again, if you and your children have enjoyed this book, I'd like to ask you to leave a great review on Amazon. Reviews help others discover the book and I love knowing that I've given something to you and your family. The link is below:

http://www.amazon.com/John-Yost/e/B00GVFG8UO

Thank you so much!

John

P.S. Feel free to write me at johnnie.yost@gmail.com

Thanks again!

P.P.S. Please visit my author page below to see what new books you and your kids can enjoy together!

http://www.amazon.com/author/johnyost

Or use this QR code to go to my author page:

Printed in Great Britain
by Amazon